Journaling the Tarot

Journaling the Tarot

A Little Book

of

Big Questions

Andy Matzner, MA, LCSW

Disclaimer

This book is made available with the understanding that the author is not engaged in offering specific medical, psychological, or emotional advice. The information, ideas, and suggestions in this book are not intended to be a substitute for professional care. Each person is unique and this book cannot take those individual differences into account. The author therefore accepts no liability or responsibility for any results, outcomes, or consequences of the use of content, ideas or concepts expressed or provided in this book.

By doubting we are led to question,

by questioning we arrive at the truth.

Peter Abelard

How do we accept...that we are not our history but our unfolding journey?

James Hollis

There is no coming to consciousness without pain.

Carl Jung

The important thing is to never stop questioning.

Albert Einstein

MISS PAMELA COLMAN SMITH, FROM A
RECENT PHOTOGRAPH.

This book is dedicated to Pamela Colman Smith

Without Whom, Not

And Tallulah Rose Costa

My April Fool

Strategic questions are tools of rebellion.

Fran Peavey

Instructions

[this page intentionally left blank]

The Fool

- What message have you been ignoring?

- What skills do you need to learn? Why?

- What person or animal is your faithful companion? How can you show them your gratitude?

- When do you feel most awkward? What are you afraid people are thinking? How can you challenge those fears?

- About what do you need more information?

- Whom do you trust? Why?

- Do you trust yourself? Why or why not?

- What are you doing for fun?

- How are you being true to yourself?

- How are you expanding your horizons?

- What experience would you like to have? Why?

- What fear do you need to get over? How will you do so?

- When are you most free?

- How are you developing your ability to stay focused in the present moment?

- What object do you most need in your life right now? Why?

- Who or what do you need to release from your life?

- What role does faith play in your life?

- Who or what are you currently taking on faith?

- Who or what are you counting on for the future?

- What price are you currently paying for remaining in the status quo?

- What are you willing to risk for a better life?

- How can you connect with your inner child? Why might this be an important thing to do?

- What call have you been resisting? Why?

- What new adventure awaits? What is your next step in that direction?

- What decision do you need to make *right now*?

- What's the worst that could happen if you fail?

The Magician

- Where is your energy going?

- Who or what is draining your energy?

- Who or what gives you energy?

- How clear are your objectives?

- What is motivating you? Are your motivations based on fear or love?

- What price are you willing to pay in order to succeed?

- What is it that you really want? How will getting it fulfill you?

- What are three skills you need to develop?

- How grounded are you?

- What can you do on a daily basis to center yourself?

- How are you using your talents?

- What distractions are you tolerating?

- How do you typically sabotage yourself?

- What is a natural talent you have been neglecting? Why?

- Just because you *can* do something doesn't mean you should. What current or upcoming activity or project do you need to reconsider?

- When do your creative juices flow most freely?

- What can you do to further stimulate your creativity?

- When do you feel most connected to others? To the Universe?

- When do you feel most powerful?

- How might you to about deliberately designing a life worth living? What are its components?

- What must you accept? Why?

- What must you change? Why?

- What must you do in order to further grow? How can you free yourself from your past conditioning?

- What is it about success that frightens you? Where might the roots of those fears lie? How might you best address them?

The High Priestess

- What is the state of your emotional life?

- What therapeutic work remains to be done?

- How are you exploring your subconscious? Why might it be a good idea to seek a connection with it?

- Why would spending more time alone be beneficial?

- Why might it be true that you already know the answer to the question you have been asking?

- How can you best create a sense of calm in your life?

- What secret wisdom should you be pursuing?

- How can you deepen your knowledge of the Tarot?

- What don't you know? What is your next step?

- What are you concealing from others? Is the decision to do so empowering or weakening?

- In what current cycle do you find yourself? How can you best honor it?

- How easy is it for you to allow things to unfold naturally? What would make it easier?

- What is waiting within you to be realized? What is your next step?

- How are societal attitudes holding you back? What can you do to challenge them in order to experience more freedom?

- What can you do to free yourself from what is binding you?

- How are you managing your moods? What new skill can you learn that would be helpful?

- How can you ensure that you are fully honoring each of your emotions?

- If you were honest with yourself, what would you realize? And then what would your next step be?

- In what area of your life should you hold back?

- How aware are you of your shadow side? What might you do to connect with it? What might you learn from it?

- What is the mystery of your life?

- How are you deepening your spirituality?

The Empress

- What is coming to an end for you?

- What is necessary for you to begin?

- How are you honoring the rhythms of Mother Nature?

- How are you acting in accordance with your age?

- What do you need to remember?

- How open are you to exploring possibilities? What are you afraid of?

- About what do you need to become more patient?

- How are you honoring the mystery in your life?

- How are you honoring your intuition?

- What can you do to further develop your intuitive abilities?

- How can you best nurture yourself?

- What aspect of yourself have you been ignoring? How can you (re)integrate it into your life?

- What are you waiting for?

- How comfortable are you with being assertive? If you need to become more comfortable, what would your next step be?

- How comfortable are you with yielding to another? Why do you think that is?

- How are you exploring your subconscious world?

- How are you honoring and balancing both your feminine and masculine energies?

- What creative projects are you developing?

- How can you honor your creative side? Your sensual side? Your sexuality?

- What gift or talent is waiting to be fully expressed?

- What is something you've always wanted to do? In order to manifest it, what would be your next step?

- What are you doing to reduce your stress?

- Whom do you need to mother? Why would that be important?

- What are you most proud of in your life? Why?

- Who or what gives you a sense of stability?

The Emperor

- Who is calling the shots in your life? How do you feel about that? Is there something that needs to change?

- How woud you define "power"? How powerful do you feel? What gives you a sense of power in your life? What can you do in order to feel more powerful?

- Where is there a need for greater boundaries in your life? What must you do in order to set and maintain those boundaries?

- Is there something you need to accept in your life? Why?

- What is beginning to wither in your life that deserves more of your attention?

- What is stagnant in your life? How can you get it flowing again?

- How are you using your power to make a difference in other people's lives?

- How can you keep yourself flexible?

- What are you doing for relaxation? What could you do more of?

- What are you doing for fun? What would you like to do for fun that you're currently not doing?

- How disciplined are you? Why might it be important for you to be more disciplined? How can you develop a sense of discipline in your life?

- How are you balancing your work life and your home life?

- What aspect of your past is still determining how you make decisions in the present? What must you do in order to resolve it?

- Is there something you've been holding onto for too long? What is it? What do you ned to do in order to release it?

- What two areas of your life would it be beneficial for you to integrate?

- What is something you need to admit? To whom? How might you go about doing that? What would be the result?

- What pain have you been hiding? What is your first step toward healing?

- What is working in your life? Why is it working?

- How might you give yourself a break?

The Hierophant

- What role did organized religion play in your life when you were growing up? Was it a positive experience?

- What role does organized religion currently play in your life? Does that role need to change?

- How would you describe your relationship with God / A Higher Power?

- What are some traditions that you have incorporated into your life? How have they been beneficial?

- What role did ritual and/or ceremony play in your life when you were growing up? What role does ritual and/or ceremony currently play in your life?

- What new (or old) ritual or ceremony do you need to incorporate into your life? Why?

- How do you honor life transitions? What current life transition would it be important for you to celebrate or mark in some way?

- What past traditions have you felt a need to rebel against?

- What are you currently learning? Why?

- What do you need to learn?

- What are some of the major lessons you have learned over the course of your life?

- Who can help you learn something you really need to know?

- How are you inspiring others?

- What is something you would like to teach to other people? How might you go about doing so?

- How might your knowledge empower other people?

- Is there someone in your life that you are taking advantage of? Why?

- Is there someone in your life you need to be nicer to? Why?

- Who have been your role models? What was it about each one that was attractive or inspirational?

- Against what or whom do you need to rebel?

- How would you characterize the relationship you've had with your father? Your mother? How have those relationships influenced your life?

The Lovers

- What choice do you need to make? How will you be sure it is the right one?

- What do you need to sacrifice? Why will it be worth it?

- What dream have you had to let go of? How can you honor that loss?

- What are some significant unresolved losses in your life? What do you need to do in order to grieve appropriately for each one?

- What is a choice you have made in your life that you now regret? How can you release that sense of regret?

- What do you need to integrate in your life? How might you best do so?

- How are you connecting with others?

- Where is the passion in your life?

- What can you do in order to bring more passion into your life?

- How true are you being to yourself? What gets in the way? What is the solution?

- What is your personal philosophy?

- About what do you care deeply?

- About whom do you care deeply?

- Who or what do you value in your life? How are you honoring who/what you value on a daily basis?

- How are you paying attention to your sensual side?

- How easy is it for you to spend time by yourself? Why or why not?

- How easy is it to say "I love and accept myself."? If you are unable to speak these words or simply don't believe they are true, what must you do in order to heal? Where/from whom did you learn that you were unlovable?

- Who or what is currently tempting you (against your better judgment)? What must you do in order to resist?

- Who is ignoring you? Why do you think that is? What is your next step?

- Are any of your relationships unbalanced? What must you do to rectify the situation?

- What gift can you give yourself?

The Chariot

- What persona are you presenting to the world? How accurately does it reflect your genuine nature? How does your persona protect you?

- What emotions are you repressing? What strategy or strategies do you use for avoiding strong emotions?

- What contradictions and/or tenstions in your life are you struggling to control?

- What is distracting you?

- If you don't make any changes, where are you going to end up?

- How in touch are you with your anger?

- How can you better manage your anger?

- How can you use your anger to create something positive?

- How are you testing your abilities in the world?

- What role does discipline play in your life?

- How can you balance being disciplined with developing your flexibility?

- In what two directions are you currently being pulled? What decision must you make next to in order clarify your commitment to one over the other?

- How willing are you to consider other options?

- What difficult choice do you need to make that will allow you to move forward with your life?

- How balanced is your life? Is there something you can do to improve its balance?

- To what are you strongly committed? Why?

- What is your commitment blinding you to?

- How is your greatest strength also your greatest weakness?

- What patterns have a tendency to repeat in your life? In terms of relationships? Work? Self-care?

- What do you believe to be true? How do you know?

- Why might you need to relax a bit more? How can you best do so?

- What is your intention for the future? How will you manifest it?

Strength

- How are you making peace with an annoyance?

- Which of your inner passions do you need to express?

- What is a difficult emotion you have been struggling with? How can you best honor it so that it does not destroy you?

- How are you currently being called upon to show courage?

- Who or what should you not give up on? Why?

- How are you currently showing compassion to others in your life?

- How are you currently showing compassion to yourself?

- To whom do you need to show compassion? Why?

- Whom do you have to win over? Why?

- Whom do you love? How are you showing that love?

- About what do you need to have more faith?

- What is something you are afraid of doing? Why is it important for you to do it? What will help you face your fear?

- What is something you know to be true about yourself or your life, that you wish weren't true? What is your next step in order to either change it or accept it?

- What is a painful memory from your past that you need to make peace with?

- Whom do you need to forgive? Why? How can you best do so?

- What worries you about the future? How can you best address that worry?

- What is something you've done in your life that you had thought you couldn't do?

- What are you hiding? Why?

- What role does shame play in your life? How can you best heal?

- Was there a time in your life that you did something that initially scared you? What was the result?

- What is the source of your power?

The Hermit

- What have you been searching for? How will you know when you have found it?

- What did you need as a child that you did not receive from your parents or caregivers? How can you best address those needs now?

- What are your current needs? How are they being addressed? Is there anything you should do differently in order to better address any of them?

- What is important for you to know? Who can help you?

- As a child, who was your favorite teacher? Why?

- Currently, what is it that you are learning? From whom or what?

- How comfortable are you being alone?

- Why might it be important for you to spend more time by yourself?

- How are you misunderstood?

- How are you being introspective? Do you journal? Meditate? Walk? Analyze your dreams? What are some other ideas?

- Why might a vision-quest be an important task for you at this point in your life?

- What is your relationship with your intuition? How might you improve this relationship?

- How can you better listen to what your intuition is trying to tell you?

- How is your body communicating to you? What is it trying to tell you?

- If you could travel anywhere in the world, where would you go?

- How do you recharge your batteries? When was the last time you did so? What gets in the way? How might you address those obstacles?

- What journey do you need to take? Why?

- How are you currently teaching others?

- What would you like to share with the world? Why? How might you best do so?

- Why is it important for you to live life on your own terms?

- How aware are you regarding the influence of your past on your present-day life?

Wheel of Fortune

- What life changes are you experiencing? How well are you adapting to those changes? What would help you better adapt?

- Is there something you need to resolve? How can you best do so?

- How are you expanding your horizons?

- How clear are you about your vision for your future?

- How easily can you see "The Big Picture" of your life? What could you do in order to gain that broad perspective?

- What do you need to make peace with? How can you best do so?

- What are you resisting? What are the benefits of doing so? The costs?

- What patterns have continually repeated throughout your life? Have they caused you suffering or empowered you? What might be the origins of those patterns?

- What is a pattern that you need to break? How could you do so most effectively?

- What dream (that has been close to your heart for a long time) do you need to say goodbye to? How might you best do that?

- How is your past influencing your present?

- How did the childhoods of your parents or early caregivers influence how they treated you when you were growing up?

- How are you just like your father? Mother?

- What are three things you learned about yourself and/or the world from your mother?

- What are three things you learned about yourself and/or the world from your father?

- What are 5 life lessons you have learned?

- What are the three things you need to do in the next week in order to start to become the best possible version of yourself?

- What is ending in your life? What is beginning?

- What positive habits can you create that will remain consistent through times of change?

- How has an initially negative life event eventually led to a positive outcome?

Justice

- What important decision are you currently weighing? What will help you make your decision without regret?

- What consequences are you experiencing due to a previous action on your part?

- What do you need to do in order to be true to yourself?

- How can you best create a sense of balance in your life?

- What daily habit is it important for you to start?

- What habit no longer serves you? How can you best release it?

- What difficult conversation do you need to have?

- How are you honoring your current commitments?

- What is a new commitment you must make to yourself? Why?

- What is a commitment you need to make to another person?

- What do you need to end now? Why?

- What are you currently doing that is leading you in the direction of your long-term goals?

- What are you currently doing that will prevent you from achieving your long-term goals?

- How is guilt impacting your life? What might you do in order to release that guilt?

- What are you an example of? How does that make you feel?

- What makes you angry? How can you use that anger to make a difference in the world?

- Whom would you like to serve? Why? What would be the most fulfilling way of doing so?

- What limiting belief is holding you back? From where did you first learn it? How might you challenge it?

- For what do you need to accept responsibility?

- As you review the course of your life, how happy are you with the outcomes of the choices you have made? What can you do moving forward that will allow you to make better choices?

- Do you believe in karma? If so, how is it operating in your life?

The Hanged Man

- How are you restricted? What will set you free? What is your next step to attain that state?

- What sacrifices are you making? Why?

- To whom or what are you currently devoted? Why?

- To whom or what is it most important for you to be devoted?

- What and/or whom have you outgrown? How do you know? What is your next step?

- How are you seeking higher knowledge?

- How are you making sure you have enough time in your day to pause and reflect?

- About what might it be important to get another perspective? What could you do in order to gain that perspective?

- Where can you give up control? Why might that be a good idea?

- What do you need to surrender to? Why?

- What price are you willing to pay in order to achieve your material goals?

- About what do you need to be more patient?

- What is something you could do to challenge yourself?

- What is a new skill you need to develop? How might you best learn it?

- How is a problem you are currently experiencing actually an opportunity?

- What don't you see? What will allow you to see it?

- How long are you willing to wait for success? How will you know when to quit if it is not meant to be?

- If you don't change, what do you know is going to happen?

- What secret knowledge do you possess?

- How do people misunderstand you? Why do you think that is?

- What do you need to trust? Why?

- What are you willing to sacrifice in order to improve your spiritual well-being?

- How can you best change your perspective?

Death

- What chapter is currently closing in your life? How are you making peace with that transition?

- What chapter in your life needs to close? How can you ensure that happens?

- What losses from your past do you still need to grieve? How can you best do so?

- What pains you? Why? How can you honor that pain?

- How are you changing (as a person)?

- How comfortable are you with your own mortality? What can you do in order to become more comfortable with the fact that one day you are going to die?

- How might the acknowledgment of your own mortality inspire you to live more fully?

- What would allow you to die without regrets?

- What would you like to accomplish before you die?

- How can you best use an awareness of your mortality as your inspiration to live a full life?

- What is something you need to review?

- What are you refusing to acknowledge? Why?

- What do you need to embrace?

- How are you honoring your age? Is there something you need to accept about getting older?

- What chapter is starting in your life? How can you ensure it is a good one?

- How can you best accept the impermanence of life? How will knowing that nothing lasts forever influence your relationship with the world around you?

- To whom or what are you unnecessarily attached? What is the next step?

- What belief about yourself no longer serves you? With what can you replace it?

- How do you currently recharge your batteries? What are some of the best ways for you to do so?

- What role does purification or cleansing play in your life? Why might that be something important?

- How can you best lighten your load? How can you ensure that you keep it light moving forward?

- What should you take more seriously?

Temperance

- What do you now know to be true about your place in the world? How does that make you feel? What is your next step?

- What are your talents? How might you combine them?

- What needs to be healed? How might you best do so?

- What is out of balance in your life? How can you create a better sense of equilibrium in your life?

- How are you renewing your energy each day? Each week?

- What compromise should you make? Why is that important? What compromise shouldn't you make?

- How are you seeing the bigger picture?

- How will the integration of two opposites bring you closer to wholeness?

- Who or what must your release from your life in order to gain clarity?

- How are you pacing yourself? How can you better pace yourself?

- How can you bring a sense of moderation into your life? Why might that be a good idea?

- What do you need to perfectly time? Why? How might you do so?

- What brings you a sense of inner peace?

- How are you paying attention to each area of your life? Is there an area you have been neglecting?

- Who supports you? How?

- What has been your greatest challenge? How did you overcome it?

- What do you now understand that you didn't in the past? How is this new knowledge impacting the decisions you make?

- With whom should you join forces? Why might that be a good idea?

- How are you integrating your spirituality into your everyday life?

- How are you integrating beauty into your life? Why might this be a good idea?

- What gives you a sense of stability during difficult times?

The Devil

- Who or what is limiting you? How? What is your next step?

- How are your boundaries serving you? How are they weakening you?

- What do you crave? What are the messages that your cravings are giving you?

- Over whom or what are you obsessing? Does your obsession empower you or weaken you?

- If you had to choose an obsession, what would it be?

- What do you doubt? Why?

- What pisses you off? What can you do about it?

- How do your material possessions own you?

- How are you enslaved? What is the answer?

- How is fear shaping your life? How can you make peace with that fear so that you can move beyond it into freedom?

- How are the ghosts of your past still influencing your life?

- Are you making your decisions based out of fear or out of love? How can you be sure?

- What do you need to view with a sense of humor?

- What fear must you face? What will help you do so?

- What seems impossible? How do you know? What is your next step?

- In what life situation is it imperative for you to take the high road?

- How would you describe your relationship with anger? What are the roots of that relationship? Do you need to manage your anger in a healthier way? If so, what is your first step?

- How does power operate in your life? How much power do you have over your daily life?

- How are you empowering others? Whom would you like to empower? Why?

- What are you doing to make a positive difference in the lives of others?

- For what do you need to accept full responsibility? What is your next step?

The Tower

- When and where was the last time you had an epiphany? What was it?

- What part of your environment do you need to restructure? How can you best do so?

- What is breaking up in your life?

- What do you need to immediately release?

- Where is the freedom in your life?

- When was the last time you were blind-sided? What happened? How did you recover?

- How is your ego getting in the way?

- Who and how would you be if you gave yourself the freedom to be spontaneous?

- How is your past limiting you?

- What are the differences between your authentic self and the persona you present to the world?

- What does liberation look like? Feel like?

- How can increase your feeling of liberation?

- What supports do you have during tough times?

- How do you keep from getting overwhelmed?

- If you do become overwhelmed, what can you tell yourself that would help?

- How can you best connect with your sense of humility?

- Who or what do you need to unmask? Why?

- Why might it be a good idea to travel more?

- If you had to plan an adventure for yourself, what would it look like?

- How did your home environment as a child influence your adult self?

- Which of your needs were not met as a child? What can you do now to begin to fulfill those needs?

- What assumption is fueling your ambition?

- Do you have a safety net? If not, how might you go about creating one?

- Which of your beliefs about yourself and the world around you must you question?

The Star

- What is your greatest hope?

- Who inspires you? What inspires you?

- How are you currently being an example to others?

- What would you like to be an example of in the future? Why is that important?

- What gift do you bring to the world? How are people responding to the way that you are using it?

- How can you avoid being a cautionary tale?

- What should people know about you?

- How are you finding serenity?

- How are you being grateful? How can you best incorporate a sense of gratitude into your life?

- How are you listening to your intuition?

- How are you following your heart?

- What is taking up the majority of your attention?

- How can you best gain clarity?

- What is your vision for the future? What is your next step on your journey to manifesting it?

- Who or what gives you faith?

- Who or what gives you strength?

- How can you ensure that you are focusing on what matters most?

- What emotional work remains to be done? What is your next step?

- How can best honor each of your senses?

- Who or what will lead you to the answers you seek?

- What can no one every take away from you?

- How are you a survivor?

- How can you celebrate or honor yourself for a recent challenge that you have overcome?

- What gives your life meaning?

- Who or what makes you smile?

- What grudge is it time to release? How might you best go about doing so?

The Moon

- What are you assuming?

- What do you fear?

- What *should* you fear?

- What is confusing you? How might you gain clarity?

- What cycle or pattern are you repeating? When did it start? Does it need to end? What is your next step?

- How have you been disillusioned?

- What is the most effective way for you to listen to your soul? How can you best honor its message?

- To whom or what are you faithful? Why?

- How have you been deceiving yourself? How can you break the trance?

- How are you grounding yourself?

- Who were you before you were socially conditioned?

- About what must you be vigilant?

- What can you do to explore the depths of your psyche? Why might this be a good idea?

- How can you honor your past struggles?

- What is distracting you? Why? What is the solution?

- How can you avoid getting distracted in the future?

- How would you describe your shadow side?

- How can you best honor your shadow?

- What journey do you need to take? Why?

- What will lead you to The Truth?

- At what stage are you in your personal evolution? What is the next step?

- At what crossroads do you stand? What information do you need in order to know which path is right for you?

- How are you missing the point?

- What bothers you about other people? How might your feelings be a projection of an aspect of your own personality?

- Who or what are you idealizing?

The Sun

- What are you proud of?

- What is an accomplishment you need to celebrate?

- What has been your greatest creation?

- What is the most important thing you know?

- How are you honoring your true self?

- What joys are you sharing with others?

- What gives you strength in difficult times?

- Who or what drains your energy?

- Who or what gives you energy?

- What are your favorite activities?

- What do you look forward to each day?

- What are you ready to birth?

- What is your grand plan?

- What makes you feel alive?

- What is your super power? How do you know?

- What do you now know to be true?

- What must you share with the world?

- What is the smallest gift you can give yourself? What would be the greatest gift you could give yourself?

- Why might it be important for you to be more spontaneous?

- What were some of your favorite activities as a child? How could you revisit them now as an adult? Why might that be a good idea?

- How are your core values aligned with the life you are currently leading? Does anything need to change?

- What is working in your life? How can you remind yourself of these things during difficult times?

- Where will your liberation come from?

- What should you be saying "Yes!" to? Why?

- What foods make you feel energized? How can you find the foods that give you good energy?

- Where is your "happy place"? How can you access it more often?

Judgement

- What have you been ignoring that you know you need to pay attention to? What is your next step?

- What does it mean "to be called"? How are you yourself being called? How are you following through on that call? What might be the price of ignoring that call?

- To whom or what are you attracted? Why?

- What are you craving? What might be behind those desires? Is there another way to fulfill them?

- How are you being distracted? What is the purpose of the distraction?

- Whom do you need to forgive? How might you best do so?

- How are you taking a stand? Is there a cause you would like to support? Why?

- How are you rallying others to your side?

- What are you now aware of? What are the implications of that new awareness?

- How aware are you of your needs? How can you best address each one?

- How might you think outside the box to solve a pressing problem?

- What behavior or way of thinking are you ready to shed? What will you replace it with?

- Is there something in your life you need to purify? How might you do so?

- How can you best rejunvenate yourself?

- What makes life worth living?

- Who is your guru? Why?

- How are you following your heart?

- How are you incorporating spirituality into your daily life?

- What long-dormant aspect of your life needs to re-emerge? Why?

- Do you feel whole? If not, how might you best achive that state?

- How are you balancing your energies?

- Is there an aspect of your life or personality that you are ashamed of? How might you release that shame?

The World

- What loose ends do you need to tie up? How?

- What journey has come to an end? How might you celebrate or honor that ending?

- How might you turn your limitations into advantages?

- What are you doing to break free of what limits you?

- What is a gift you can give your body?

- How can you feel more satisfied with life?

- How are you practicing mindfulness? What new mindfulness habit might you add to your life?

- How might you best integrate your various interests and personalities?

- What does it feel like to "be whole"?

- How would you define "masculine" and "feminine"? How are you balancing your masculine and feminine energies?

- How are you taking into account the bigger picture?

- What would you like your next adventure to be? Why? What is your next step to manifest it?

- How will adding more structure to your life free up your creativity?

- How can you become more spontaneous?

- How can you best break a destructive pattern?

- What can you do to gain a broader perspective? Where might you go to do so?

- How present are you in your daily life? What can you do to develop your ability to remain in the "here and now"?

- What new chapter needs to begin in your life? How can you best proceed?

- What is your strategy to avoid getting caught up in the pettiness of life?

- What do you now understand? What are the implications of that understanding?

- What is the meaning of life? What is the meaning of *your* life?

- How would you treat your body if you believed it were sacred?

Ace of Wands

- Who or what is currently inspiring you?

- Where do you go or what do you do for inspiration?

- How can you best express your creativity?

- Where is your energy going? Is there anyplace it especially needs to go? How might you direct it there?

- What fear do you need to face? Why?

- How are you procastinating? What purpose does it serve?

- What new opportunity is being offered to you? How can you avoid sabotaging yourself?

- What is your gut telling you?

- What new direction should you be following?

- What are your favorite ways to express yourself creatively?

- What creative pursuits did you engage in as a youngster or adolescent? Why did you stop?

- How can you best nourish your creative spirit?

- What is beginning to blossom in your life?

- What are five creative projects you've always wanted to do?

- What is something you've always wanted to learn?

- What gift is life offering you?

- What do you have to change in your life in order to make the time and space in which you are free to explore your creativity?

- What price are you willing to pay to manifest your creative spirit?

- With whom might you share your creative expression?

- What are some beliefs you have regarding your creative spirit? Are they empowering or do they limit you?

- What kinds of things does your inner critic tell you? How can you challenge that voice?

- Is your environment fertile ground for growth? If not, what are your options?

- What desire are you repressing? Why?

Two of Wands

- Where do you see yourself in a year? 5 years? 10 years? What steps must you take now in order to move in those directions?

- What conflicting desires do you need to integrate?

- What two ideas can you bring together in a new and interesting way?

- At what threshold do you stand? What is your next step?

- What possible futures lay before you? Which of those paths will bring you the most fulfillment and the least amount of regret?

- How are you using your influence? How would you ideally like to be using your influence in the future?

- What do you see that others don't?

- What must you put aside (for now)?

- What is the big picture? Do you see it clearly?

- What trend do you see on the horizon?

- What skill do you need to learn or develop more fully in order to achieve your heart's desire? What would have to be your first step in that direction?

- About what do you need more clarity? What can you do that will provide it?

- What creative pursuit must you prioritize over others?

- What price are you willing to pay for success?

- How are you holding back? Why might you be doing so?

- What aspects of success frighten you?

- What resoures are you lacking? How can you best gain them?

- What is your vision for your creative potential? Who can help you manifest it?

- What is your backup plan?

- What about you is unique?

- What is your secret weapon? How can you best use it?

- How would you describe your creative process? Does something need to change about it?

- Where do you have to go to find success?

Three of Wands

- What are your regrets?

- What opportunities have you missed?

- How are you feeling misunderstood?

- How are you ahead of your time?

- What is your relationship with solitude?

- Do you gain energy from being alone or around people?

- Will your creativity flourish in isolation or in community?

- What price are you willing to pay to set your own course?

- Which of your creative gifts are lying dormant? How might you awaken them?

- What resources are you ignoring? How can you best access them?

- What are you most proud of?

- What gives you a sense of satisfaction?

- What do you now understand that you didn't in the past?

- What has been the biggest obstacle you've ever faced? How did you overcome it?

- How can you best combine your talents?

- How will changing your perspective diminish your suffering?

- What must you master in order to move forward in life?

- What must you do in order to see more clearly? Does this clarity come with a price?

- What can you do in order to gain the experience you need in order to grow?

- What pilgrimage must you make? Why?

- What obstacles stand in the way of you being able to express your creative potential? What is your plan for overcoming them?

- How do you feel about leading others? Why might you be suited for that role?

- How can you learn about future trends? How might you best take advantage of them?

Four of Wands

- What are you bringing to completion?

- What role does ritual or ceremony play in your life?

- What ritual do you need to perform? Why? What would it consist of?

- How might a regularly occurring ritual or ceremony improve the quality of your life?

- What needs to become integrated into your life?

- What should you be celebrating? How can you best do so?

- What or whom do you need to honor?

- What are you looking forward to?

- What do you need to release?

- What rite of passage is still waiting to be celebrated? How might you best do so?

- What is it time to finally harvest so that the ground might rest?

- Why might it be a good idea to settle down?

- How can you best share your creative output with others?

- With whom would you like to collaborate?

- What door must you walk through? Why? What might prevent you from doing so?

- Who or what is calling out to you? What is your best response?

- How are you isolating yourself? What are you afraid of? How might you face that fear?

- How are you balancing solitude with community?

- How are you balancing your active and passive energies?

- Who or what are you ignoring?

- Which aspects of your creativity give you the most satisfaction?

- Who or what gives you the strength to complete your creative projects?

- Why might it be a good idea to hibernate?

- How can you set up your home to be a place of refuge?

Five of Wands

- With whom are you competing? Why?

- What are you agonizing over? How might you resolve the issue once and for all?

- What isn't going according to plan? How might you get back on track?

- How are you being pulled in different directions? What do you need to say "no" to or release?

- How are you paying attention to details?

- What are you having a hard time getting off the ground? What would make it easier?

- About what do you need clarity? What do you need to do in order to gain that clarity?

- How are you extending yourself too thin? What must you do about it to preserve yourself?

- How might you simplify your life?

- What do you need to prioritize? Why? What could get in the way?

- What projects do you need to put on the back-burner?

- How are you getting in your own way? What must you do in order to become more aware of how you sabotage yourself?

- How can you begin to become more disciplined? How might this aid your creativity?

- How are you distracting yourself? Why?

- What should you be taking more seriously?

- How are you having fun?

- What would be something fun to try that you've never done before?

- What was something fun you used to do that is no longer a part of your life? How might you reintroduce it?

- How are you balancing work and play? How are you balancing work and family?

- How curious are you? How might you stimulate your curiosity?

- How are you being paralyzed by an abundance of choices? Why can you do to make it easier to choose once and for all?

- How can you best get noticed?

Six of Wands

- What kind of leadership do others need from you? How are you developing yourself as a leader? Which current or past leader is your role model?

- How are others recognizing your accomplishments?

- How important is it for you to receive validation from others? Why?

- How are you managing your pride? How can you ensure it doesn't turn into arrogance?

- Who might betray you? How can you protect yourself?

- What or whom are you overlooking?

- What are you proud of? What are you *most* proud of? Why?

- To whom should you be giving credit?

- Whom do you admire? Why?

- What is your definition of success?

- How are you successful?

- What gives you a sense of satisfaction?

- How would you describe your self-esteem? What is it based on? What might be some other ways to connect with a sense of self-worth?

- What do you love most about yourself?

- What is the elephant in the room? What must you do about it? Why?

- Which of your foundations needs to be strengthened? How can you best do so?

- Who or what could hurt you? How can you best protect yourself?

- What detail should you be paying closer attention to?

- What could undermine your self-confidence?

- How might you be pissing someone off? Is that a good thing or a bad thing?

- How can ensure that your success is permanent?

- How can you avoid comparing yourself to others?

- How does your ego influence your decision-making?

- How can you learn to put your ego to the side?

Seven of Wands

- Who or what is competing for your attention? Your time? How can you best create healthy boundaries in order to protect yourself?

- How are you being true to yourself? Who or what gets in the way? What can you do about it?

- How can you better assert yourself?

- How strong are your boundaries? Are there any boundaries that you need to strengthen? Why?

- What is your philosophy of life?

- What is your life's mission? How are you honoring that mission each day?

- Who or what are you resisting? Why?

- What did you forget to do? How can you ensure that you remember to do it in the future?

- Is there an area in your life in which you need to slow down? How might you do so?

- How can you become more mindful?

- How are you demonstrating your value to yourself? To others?

- What are you fighting for? Why?

- What priorities do you need to set? How will you decide what is most important?

- How are you choosing what to focus on? Are you satisfied with your choices?

- How are you protecting your time?

- How are you rejunvenating yourself?

- Who or what is draining your energy? How can you protect yourself?

- How do you normally ground yourself when you are feeling unsettled? Do you need to learn any new techniques in this area?

- How are you being backed into a corner? What can you do to give yourself the freedom you need?

- What decision do you need to make? How is your indecisiveness hurting you?

- What are you currently tolerating in your life? Is there a step you need to take that will increase the quality of your life?

- Are you sure you know what you're doing? How can you be certain?

Eight of Wands

- What are you rushing into? How carefully have you thought it through?

- How are you putting your plans into action?

- What are you compelled to share with others? Why? How might you best do so?

- How might you complete unfinished business?

- What information or skills do you need in order to move forward?

- Where are you blocked? When did the blockage start? How might you best remove it?

- When do you feel most alive? How can you increase those experiences on a daily or weekly basis?

- How can you best manage your energy?

- How can you take advantage of those times during the day when you feel most energized?

- How are you showing up for your life mission? What gets in the way? What makes it easier?

- How are you honoring your creative spirit?

- How can you best clear the way?

- How are you avoiding what might clog up your life?

- What daily ritual can you utilize in order to feel cleansed?

- What areas of your life are sluggish? How can you get them to flow more easily?

- How are you keeping yourself grounded in the present moment?

- How are you allowing yourself to be spontaneous?

- What scares you about letting yourself be spontaneous? What can you do to face that fear?

- What can you do to prevent yourself from getting overwhelmed?

- What message do you need to send right now? To whom? Why is that important to do?

- How focused are you? On what is it vital to be focused on right now in your life?

- How are you learning to control where your attention goes? Is there a skill you need to master that would help in this area?

Nine of Wands

- Who or what inspires you?

- What are you afraid of? How can you prevent those fears from limiting you?

- How have you been hurt? What can you do to forgive? Why would such forgiveness be beneficial?

- What does your inner critic tell you? Whose voice is it? A parent's? A teacher's? How might you best dispute it?

- What are the enemies of your creativity?

- Were you supported in your creativity as a child? What happened?

- What price have you paid to be your authentic self? Have you made peace with having to pay that price?

- What has allowed you to keep your faith?

- What is your favorite quote? Why?

- What stands in the way of your success?

- What irons do you have in the fire? Which should you prioritize?

- Over what are you obsessing? Is it healthy?

- Why might it be a good idea to loosen up?

- What role does envy play in your life? How might you release it?

- What role does jealous play in your life? How might you heal from it?

- What is the one thing standing between you and success?

- What price are you willing to pay to follow your dreams?

- How have you been traumatized? How can you begin to heal?

- What are your favorite ways of self-care?

- How can you be more self-compassionate?

- What is most important from you to protect?

- What might end up being less scary than it seems? How will you know?

- What is something that, in spite of difficulties, you should pursue to the end?

Ten of Wands

- How are you over-extending yourself? How are you over-committed? What is the solution?

- Where are you experiencing resistance?

- What is weighing you down? What would it feel like without that burden? Can you imagine that for even a moment?

- What scares you about success? How can you avoid sabotaging yourself?

- How are you staying grounded?

- What do you need to pay attention to? Why?

- Who or what is preventing you from reaching your full potential?

- What is the best way to give yourself over to your muse?

- Why might it be more important to enjoy the process than be solely focused on the outcome?

- How is your creativity manifesting itself in the world?

- In what do you have complete faith? Why?

- What gives you the strength to carry on, even when times get tough?

- Where is your creativity leading you?

- How are you being called? Are you following the call? Why or why not?

- What are you tolerating in your life?

- To what in your life do you need to say "No more!"

- How might a dedication to perfection be causing you suffering?

- What is the best way to slow down and truly savor the fruits of your labor?

- Why might less be more?

- What have you been collecting? Has it been worth it?

- What responsibilities will come with your success? How does that make you feel?

- What is the gap between the fruits of your creativity and being able to share those fruits with others? How can you best close it?

Page of Wands

- What are you enthusiastic about?

- Are you feeling restless? If so, what is your next step?

- What new things are you interested in exploring?

- Who or what keeps calling you? Why do you think that is? Have you answered that call? Why or why not?

- Who is enthusiastic about you? Why?

- What new practical skill would you like to master?

- What is something you've always wanted to learn (even if has no practical applications)?

- In order to move forward in your life, whom do you have to meet? Why? How will you make that connection?

- Where do you find inspiration?

- What did you love to do as a child? How did it make you feel? How might you return to that state?

- Why might it be a good idea to join a new community?

- What message has the Universe been giving you? Have you been listening?

- What are you just itching to do? Why haven't you done it yet?

- What do you want to create? Why?

- What area of your life has withered? How can you bring new life to it?

- When was the last time you had fun? What can you do to bring more of those moments into your life?

- What is your intuition trying to communicate to you about your future?

- How might you open your third eye?

- What is the connection between spontaneity and creativity? What is the connection between discipline and creativity?

- Why might it be a good idea to incorporate more mystical experiences into your life?

- To whom should you send a message of thanks?

- How are you still acting like a child? What is behind that? Is there something you need to do about it?

Knight of Wands

- What are you obsessing over? How is that obsession serving you? How is it weakening you?

- Are you stuck in a rut? How would you know? If so, what is the solution?

- How are you getting weighed down? What is your next step?

- How is your laser-like focus helping you? Hurting you?

- What have you started too soon? How would you know if that were the case?

- How are you over-extending yourself?

- In what area of your life should you slow down a bit?

- How can you avoid getting burnt out?

- Do you have a mentor? If not, how might you find one?

- How are you honoring the seasons?

- Are you getting enough rest? If not, how might you do so?

- How clear is your plan for the future?

- What are you rushing into? Why might it be a good idea to take a time out?

- About what are you impatient? Why? What are you afraid of?

- Where does your strength come from? How might you protect it?

- How can you ensure that your excitement about a new project doesn't fade?

- What should you stop resisting and just accept? What can you tell yourself to make it easier?

- How willing are you to throw caution to the wind? Why?

- How are you a pioneer? What new ground are you breaking?

- What is your dream? How will you feel once you've achieved it? Why?

- Whom do you need to challenge? Why?

- About what are you absolutely sure? What is something you used to think was true but now know isn't?

Queen of Wands

- What gives you a feeling of satisfaction?

- What are you a master of? What was that journey like?

- Do you remember the last time you felt confident? What can you do to easily access that state (physically and mentally) when it is called for?

- How are you sharing your gifts with others?

- How balanced is your life? What can you do to create even more of a sense of balance?

- Who protects you? How?

- How are you still finding time for play?

- How are you exploring – and making peace with – your shadow side?

- How connected are you with others in your area(s) of interest? Why might it be a good idea to "be in the loop" by becoming a part of those kinds of communities?

- How are you giving yourself permission to be spontaneous? Why is becoming more spontaneous a good idea for you?

- What can you do to become more mindful and situated in the present moment?

- What can you do that will allow you to think outside the box?

- Are you paying attention to the big picture? Why might this be a good idea?

- What do you need to root out of your life? Why?

- How are you balancing solitude and connections with others?

- How are you balancing work and leisure?

- How are you protecting your creative spark?

- How can you best use your gifts for social justice?

- Whom would you be interested in mentoring?

- What have your experiences taught you?

- What challenge are you ready to face? What will give you the strength necessary to prevail?

- With whom should you ally yourself? Why?

- What friendship are you overlooking?

King of Wands

- What have you created? What is next?

- Do you feel in control of your life? If not, what do you need to do to rectify the situation?

- How connected are you to your personal power? What gets in the way? How can you best manifest the power that lays within you?

- Whom do you respect? Why?

- What are you currently an example of? Ideally, what would you like to be an example of?

- What makes you angry? How might you use that anger to make a difference in the world?

- What would you like your legacy to be?

- Does being a leader scare you? Why? Why not?

- Are you successfully managing your energy? If not, how might you do so?

- How has single-mindedness served you? How might it be a liability?

- Where does your commitment lie? What are you doing about it?

- What must you do? Why?

- What has been your greatest obstacle? How did you overcome it?

- What adventures do you remember fondly?

- What are your regrets?

- How might you begin to live your life so that when you're on your deathbed you'll look back with minimal regret?

- What makes you feel powerful? What makes you feel alive?

- How are you demonstrating your value to others?

- How can you ensure that you won't get bored?

- Are any of your expectations too high? If so, what might be more reasonable?

- In what area of your life should you show a bit more restraint?

- Is a lack of progress frustrating you? If so, what is the remedy?

- Imagine you are on your deathbed. Looking back, what was it that made your life worth living?

Ace of Cups

- What relationships are beginning to flower in your life? What do they offer you?

- How connected are you with your emotions?

- What do you do to distract yourself from painful or overwhelming emotions (positive or negative)? Are your strategies effective? Why or why not?

- Who or what makes you smile?

- Whom or what do you love with all of your heart?

- What can you do in order to beter recognize your emotions and, having done so, allow them to flow unimpeded through you?

- How easy is it for you to sit still and just notice how you are feeling?

- When are you happiest?

- Who or what fills you with positive energy?

- Who or what drains your energy?

- How do you define spirituality?

- What is your spiritual life like?

- How do you connect with your higher power or the Universe?

- What spiritual practice would you like to develop? Why?

- How connected are you with your subconscious? How can you further develop that connection?

- What message is your intuition giving you? How are you honoring that message?

- What have your dreams been telling you? Why do you think that is?

- How can you protect yourself from overwhelming emotions?

- How can you best protect yourself from being traumatized by the pain of others?

- How can you best protect your heart?

- What lessons have you learned from your pain?

- Where does your shame lie? Where does it come from? How might you heal?

- What is your gift? How can you best share it with others?

Two of Cups

- Whom do you need to nurture? How might you best do so?

- What are you sharing with others? What would you like to share with others?

- Whom do you need to forgive? How might you do that?

- What alliance should you be making?

- Whom do you need to contact?

- What emotion do you need to fully process and then release?

- What do you need to be open to receiving?

- In what area of your life do you need to take the first step?

- How is pride or fear preventing you from reaching out?

- What two aspects of your life or personality do you need to integrate?

- What painful event from your past do you need to make peace with so that it will stop haunting you?

- What new relationships are blossoming in your life?

- How can you best expand your circle of friends?

- To whom or what is it finally time to make a commitment?

- How can you best open your heart to another while at the same time protecting it?

- How is being vulnerable the key to your healing?

- What can you do to bring a state of balance to your life?

- What relationship do you need to defend?

- How are you balancing solitude and being with others?

- What current relationship is over? How do you know? What is your next step?

- What would it be like to become your own best friend? Why might that be important?

- How might you better develop your sense of empathy?

- In whose shoes is it important for you to walk to gain a sense of their struggles and hopes?

Three of Cups

- Where is the joy in your life?

- What do you need to celebrate?

- How strong is your community or friendship circle? Does it need strengthening? How might you do that?

- Have you found your tribe yet? If not, what must you do?

- How are you being grateful for what you have?

- What is the toughest thing you have ever done? How can you honor that accomplishment?

- How are you savoring life?

- Who or what gives you joy?

- How are you setting aside time for fun?

- How are you holding back? What are you afraid of?

- Is there an area in your life in which you are hesistant to stand out? Why?

- What is preventing you from fully manifesting your personal power?

- Do you care what other people think? Why?

- How comfortable are you being the center of attention? What would make you feel more comfortable?

- Who is your support group? Whom do you turn to when times get tough?

- When have you felt most alive?

- Whom would you like to support?

- How are you poised for leadership?

- Are you ready to make a splash? Why is that something you might need to do?

- How are you sharing your gifts? Is there a particular group that especially needs what you have to offer?

- With whom are you willing to be vulnerable? How might this lead to healing?

- Is there something you are overlooking?

- How can you ensure that you don't let your emotions get in the way of an important relationship?

- Have you ever felt on the outside looking in? What was that experience like?

Four of Cups

- Where do you go to find peace?

- What do you need to retreat from?

- How are you setting aside time to be alone?

- How comfortable are you spending time alone or in reflection?

- How do you recharge your batteries? What are some other ways that sound appealing?

- Do you currently engage in any mindfulness or contemplative practices? If not, why do you think it might be beneficial to do so?

- How can you best resist temptations or cravings that do not serve you?

- What do you need to re-evaluate?

- How are you dissatisfied? What can you do about it?

- What or who no longer excites you?

- What blessings are you ignoring?

- What gift are you refusing? Why?

- What emotion(s)s are you repressing? What is the price you are paying for doing so?

- How are you managing your emotions? Is there a new skill you could learn that would help?

- How are you taking your dreams (both waking and sleeping) seriously?

- What would you rather forget? Why?

- What or whom should you be paying more attention to?

- Who is ignoring you? What does it mean? What should you do about it?

- Do you feel the world is receptive to what you have to offer? If not, what is your next step?

- What is it time to finally admit?

- What popular trend should you be paying more attention to?

- When is it beneficial to be stubborn? When is being so a liability?

- How are you missing out?

- What role has rejection played in your life?

Five of Cups

- What is awaiting your attention?

- What still needs to be resolved?

- What or whom are you ignoring that could help?

- What have you learned?

- What is your experience with death and dying?

- What role has grief and mourning played in your life?

- What do you need to grieve? How might you give yourself the permission you need to do so?

- Why might it be a good idea to set aside time by yourself in order to get in touch with repressed emotions?

- How can you best honor the losses you have experienced in your life?

- What role does hope play in your life?

- How can you ensure that ghosts from your past do not influence the decisions you make in the present?

- Whom or what do you need to exorcise from your life? What would that ritual look like? How do you imagine you would feel afterwards?

- What resources are you ignoring?

- What chapter needs to close in your life? What can you do to welcome a new one?

- What do you take for granted in your life? For what or whom should you express your gratitude?

- What role does self-pity play in your life? Why might it need to change?

- How can you connect on a more regular basis with what makes you feel alive?

- What happens when you step back and look at the bigger picture?

- What fact do you need to accept about your life?

- Are you feeling fulfilled professionally? If not, can you imagine what your ideal scenario would be? What first step can you take to move in that direction?

- *What you focus on, grows*. What are you currently focusing on? Does it empower you or weaken you?

Six of Cups

- How are you sharing your joy with others?

- How do you distract yourself from strong emotions? How effective are those strategies?

- How are you listening to your emotions? What are they guiding you to do or be?

- How are you exploring the roots of your emotional life? Why might that be a good idea?

- How willing are you to be fully present with your emotions as they come up? What gets in the way? How might you best learn to be present and allow yourself to experience emotions so that you can process them fully?

- What pleasant memories do you have from childhood? What are you nostalgic for? Why?

- What are some painful memories from childhood? How might you heal the pain that you still carry with you about what happened?

- On whom or what are you wasting your energy? What is the best next step for you?

- How easy is it for you to access your inner child or inner chidren? What would make it easier? Why might this be a good idea?

- What message(s) does your inner child have for you?

- Is there an aspect of you from the past (that is, an inner child) that still needs healing or reassurance? How might you best provide it?

- How were you betrayed as a child? What must you now do in order to heal?

- Which of your childhood needs were not met? How can you best meet them now as an adult?

- Where do you belong? If you are not yet there, how can you make sure you arrive sooner than later?

- How are you feeling blessed?

- Why might it be important to re-experience your innocence and freedom? By what means could you best do so?

- What secret from your childhood do you still carry with you? Is that secret a burden? If so, what must you do release it?

- What unfinished business from your past do you still have? How can you resolve it?

- What are you missing? Who can give it to you?

- What difference will you make in the world?

Seven of Cups

- How are you indulging youself? What are the pros and cons?

- What are you doing to excess? What do you think is behind your behavior?

- What is on your mind when you first wake up in the morning? What is the last thing you are thinking about before you fall asleep?

- What is captivating you? Over what are you obsessing?

- **Sight. Hearing. Touch. Taste. Smell.** How are you gratifying each of your senses?

- How might discipline be your ally?

- Is there a goal you have that is stalled because you are overwhelmed? How might you best move forward?

- What are your options? What will allow you to choose wisely?

- What option is it time to release? Why?

- What is your definition of success? How many different definitions can you come up with?

- What does success feel like? Is there anything you can do right now that will give you the same or similar feeling?

- What role does money play in your life? What role *should* it play?

- Where is your focus? Is it justified?

- How are you being distracted? How can you break the trance?

- What are your top three goals in life? How clear are you about your motivations for each one?

- How are you being true to yourself? How can you ensure that you remain true to yourself as you progress in life?

- What role does spirituality play in your life?

- Is there an area in your life where you definitely should not be cutting corners? Why?

- How is your imagination an ally?

- Who is making life decisions for you? How does that make you feel?

- What fantasy is it time to abandon? Why?

- What would your three wishes be?

Eight of Cups

- What hopeless situation do you need to remove yourself from? How might you best do so?

- Imagine you were going on a quest...what would the goal of that quest be?

- What no longer fulfills you? What can you do about it?

- What is it time to change in your life?

- How are you exploring your subconscious?

- At what stage of life are you? What ritual can you create to celebrate or honor entering that stage?

- What aspect of your life do you need to heal? What is your first step?

- What parts of your past must you explore and resolve in order to move forward?

- What does the word "pilgrimage" mean to you? Why might it be relevant to your life at this time?

- Where do you usually go for answers? Why? What new place should you try?

- If you were to design the perfect retreat for yourself, what would it consist of?

- How do you know you are going in the right direction?

- What old habits do you need to change? What would be your plan for doing so?

- What from your past no longer serves you? How can you best release what needs to go?

- How do you recharge your batteries? How often do you do so?

- What bores you?

- How can you create a deeper sense of meaning in your life?

- What are your spiritual goals?

- Who or what has disappointed you in the past?

- Who or what is currently disappointing you? What is your next step?

- Which of your material possessions is it time to let go of? How might you do so?

- What should you re-dedicate yourself to? Why?

- What would an "emotional cleansing" look like? Why might that be a good idea?

Nine of Cups

- How satisfied are you – *truly*?

- How are you enjoying what you already have?

- How do you relax?

- What are you hiding? How might this secret be draining your life energy?

- What don't you see that everyone else does?

- What are you missing?

- How are you preventing your personal growth?

- Who or what are you proud of?

- A year from now, what would you like to be proud of?

- How would you describe your emotional intelligence? How aware are you of your feelings? How do you typically handle them when they arise?

- Emotionally, how far have you come in your life?

- What is the elephant in the room?

- What fulfills you?

- About what do you feel confident? About what should you feel more confident?

- How connected are you to your heart? How might you deepen that connection in a positive way?

- Are there certain emotions you avoid? Why? What is the price for doing so?

- Is there a certain emotion or feeling you would like to connect more with in your life? Why do you think it has been lacking? What can you do to experience it more regularly?

- Do you ever find yourself stuck in your head? How can you best get back into your body when that happens?

- How might your pride be getting in the way of your personal growth?

- What are your top five accomplishments?

- How do you deal with strong emotions? Which of your strategies for doing so are helpful? Which are destructive?

- What is your heart's desire? Why?

- For whom or what are you grateful?

Ten of Cups

- Whom do you love? How do you show your love?

- Where do you currently find joy? Where have you found joy in the past?

- How is your relationship with each of your family members?

- Are you aware of all of your different selves? How can you best honor and/or integrate them into your life?

- How are you living in harmony with your environment?

- What should you acknowledge? What should you celebrate?

- How are you showing gratitude?

- How will you know when you've finally arrived?

- What gives you energy?

- To whom are you attracted?

- What would make your home life perfect?

- What is the meaning of life?

- What are five fanstasies that you have?

- What is the state of your creative life? How can you foster it?

- How can you best reconcile your inner and outer worlds?

- How can you best create or maintain a sense of balance in your life?

- What journey are you currently on? How will you know when you've reached its conclusion?

- What is your ideal home?

- What is your ideal family situation like?

- How is your reality getting in the way of your deams?

- How are your dreams getting in the way of your reality?

- About what should you take a more pragmatic approach?

- What are the benefits of making peace with your current life situation?

- What does it mean to you to be "mentally healthy"?

Page of Cups

- Where is your heart leading you? How are you listening?

- How is your greatest strength also your greatest weakness?

- Whom do you trust? Is your trust well-founded?

- How easy is it for you to recognize what you are truly feeling? What do you need to do about feeling?

- What strategies do you use to manage your emotions? What is something that would be helpful for you to learn?

- Whom do you love? How can you best show your love to others?

- How would you describe your emotional life?

- What aspect of your emotional life frightens you? What do you need to do in order to manage that aspect in a healthy way?

- Who or what brings tears to your eyes?

- Why might it be a good idea to begin to explore your subconscious?

- How are you paying attention to your dreams?

- What new project are you excited about?

- Is there something you've been ignoring? Why?

- How in touch are you with your intuition? How can you strengthen that relationship?

- Think about how and why you typically make choices in your life...How can you learn to make decisions based on love rather than fear?

- What is something you've been afraid of doing? Why? What can you tell yourself that will allow you to move forward?

- What can you do to re-experience the child-like wonder you once had?

- What do you need to see with fresh eyes?

- What message do you have for the world? Why is it important for you to be the one spreading it?

- Why might it be a good idea to do something that is totally out of character for you?

- How can you best appreciate the little things in life?

- About what do you need to be more mature?

Knight of Cups

- What role does romance play in your life?

- If you took yourself out on a date, where would you go?

- In what creative way can you express your love for life?

- In what creative way can you express your pain?

- What does it mean to you to have a life "in balance"?

- How balanced is your life? If it is unbalanced, what can you do improve things?

- What does it mean to "live fully"?

- How are you living fully? What gets in the way of you living fully?

- How do you protect your heart?

- How aware are you of the moods and energies of those around you? How is that awareness a gift? How is it destructive?

- How are you spending time in introspection?

- What are you doing to grow as a person? What could you do more of?

- How can you protect yourself from being traumatized by the pain that exists in the world?

- How are you paying attention to what makes life special?

- How are you demonstrating your love to those around you?

- How do you exercise your imagination?

- How can you avoid taking things personally?

- When you feel depressed, what can you do to feel better?

- How willing are you to listen to the message that depression is giving you?

- How can you best balance the spiritual with the worldly?

- How are you surrounding yourself with beauty? Why is that important?

- What are you about to do? Have you prepared well?

- What action is it time to take? Why?

Queen of Cups

- Is there still any emotional work left for you to do? What has gotten in the way of you doing that work? Why is it important for you to do that work? What next step must you take in order to move forward?

- When do you feel most loved?

- When are you most loving?

- How easy is it for you to accept yourself unconditionally? If it is difficult or impossible, what can you do to begin to move in the direction of self-acceptance?

- What does it mean to be compassionate? How can you show yourself more compassion?

- Why is patience a virtue? About what should you be more patient?

- How sensitive are you to the needs of others? What can you do to develop that sensitivity? How can you ensure a balance between meeting other people's needs and taking care of your own?

- Is it easy for you to say "No"? If it is difficult, what are you afraid of? What can you tell yourself that will make it easier for you to say "No" when it is appropriate?

- How do you connect with the world around you? How would you ideally like to connect with the world around you?

- What role does spirituality play in your life? Is there a spiritual practice you would like to develop? What would be the first step to doing so?

- How connected are you to your unconscious? What can you do to further develop that connection?

- How easy is it for you to *respond* rather than *react* to emotional triggers?

- How willing are you to honor your moods, whether joyful or painful?

- How can you best defend yourself from the toxic energy that you pick up from other people?

- How are you spending time on self-care?

- What gift can you give yourself?

- How are you creating and maintaining healthy boundaries? Why might that be important?

- What are you bottling up? Why?

- Is there something you feel guilty about? If so, how can you resolve it?

King of Cups

- What advice would you give your younger self?

- What do you know to be true about yourself? Other people? The world?

- To whom might you be a mentor?

- What five lessons has life taught you?

- In what area of your life is patience called for? Why?

- How are you exposing yourself to different viewpoints? Why might this be a good idea?

- How are you sharing your gifts with others?

- How are you making a difference in the world? How does that make you feel?

- What makes you angry? How might you use that anger to create change?

- Why might it be a good idea to seek out a mentor?

- Is there a type of volunteer service you would be interested in doing? What is it about that service that resonates with you? What would be the first step you'd need to take in order to make it happen?

- How are you attending to the emotional needs of those around you? How are you attending to your own emotional needs?

- What role does compassion play in your life?

- How do you keep yourself grounded in difficult situations? Is there a particular skill you need to learn in order to develop that ability?

- What kind of leader are you?

- What would be important for you to teach to others?

- What is your relationship with your emotions? How might you strengthen that relationship?

- Do you feel that you have done the necessary emotional/healing work that you've had to do? If not, what is getting in the way? Why is it important for you to do that work?

- How can you help two opposing sides to come together? Why might benefit you as well?

- How might you be able to accept more responsibility for your life?

- What are the next three things you would need to do in order to take charge of your life? What are you waiting for?

Ace of Swords

- What is on your mind? What, if anything, do you need to do about it?

- What do you need to analyze more deeply? Why?

- What decision must you make? Why is it a good idea to move forward with it instead of procrastinating further?

- What truth is slowly dawning on you? What do you know in your heart that you need to do about it?

- What is something that you are afraid to do? What messages are you telling yourself that keep you stuck in fear? What might you tell yourself instead to successfully challenges those fears?

- How are you distracting yourself from what is important? Why might you be doing that? What do you need to do next to liberate yourself?

- What do you need to clarify?

- What questions should you be asking?

- What decision could come back to haunt you later?

- What is something you need to do more of? Less of? What is something you need to start? Stop?

- Consider your internal dialogue...What do you tell yourself that limits you? That makes you feel "less than"? That makes you feel badly about yourself? Where did you learn those limiting beliefs? With what empowering messages could you replace them?

- Who or what is holding you back from your potential to be become the best version of yourself? Based on your answers, what must you do next

- Does your self-talk create liberation or suffering?

- To what or whom are you committed? Why?

- How do you keep your mind sharp?

- What new things are you learning? Why might it be a good idea to be a life-long learner?

- How are your emotions holding you back from a decision you know you need to make?

- What isn't adding up?

- Who will you champion? Why?

- What has gotten out of hand? How can you set matters straight again?

- Who or what would you be willing to die for? Why?

Two of Swords

- What is confusing you? What must you do in order to gain the clarity you need?

- What difficult decision is before you? How might you best make it?

- How are you protecting your heart? Why is this a good idea? Why might this sometimes cause you regret?

- What feelings are you repressing? Why?

- Why might it be a good idea to do some deep emotional work?

- What is causing you stress? What must you do in order to manage it?

- What are you refusing to see? Why might this be a bad idea?

- How are you being pulled in two different directions?

- How have you been hurt in the past? Have you healed that wound? How might it still be impacted you today?

- What is becoming unsustainable or unbearable in your life? What is your next step?

- According to an old Russian proverb, a dog that chases two rabbits catches neither. How does this apply to your situation? What decision must you make in order in order to move forward?

- About what do you need to loosen up?

- How can you incorporate more spontaneity into your life?

- To whom should you apologize? Why?

- Who or what in your life deserves a second look?

- What belief do you have that no longer serves you? That limits your potential? That keeps you stuck? What empowering belief or statement might you replace it with?

- About what do you need to be more flexible?

- Why must you pay more attention to your feelings?

- How attentive are you to your energy flow? Why might this be important?

- How do you see the world? From where or whom did you learn this way of seeing? Does your perspective empower you or limit you?

- With whom do you need to make a truce?

Three of Swords

- How might your emotions be leading you down the wrong path?

- How are you balancing logic with emotion?

- What are you keeping bottled up inside? How can you best release it?

- What do you need to purify in your life? How might you do so?

- What loss from your past still needs to be fully mourned? How can you best do that?

- Whom do you need to forgive? Why?

- What is your action plan for self-growth?

- What are past hurts that still carry an emotional charge? How can you heal them so that you can move forward unencumbered?

- How is fear preventing you from doing something you know you need to do?

- How can you honor the suffering you have experienced? What artistic work can you create? What ritual or ceremony can you plan?

- What sacrifice must you make? Why?

- With whom do you need to have a clarifying conversation? Why is that necessary?

- How have you been betrayed? What do you need to do in order to heal from what happened?

- What suffering are you avoiding? How might fully experiencing that pain actually lead to healing?

- How have you been beating around the bush? Why is a more direct approach a better course of action?

- Who or what has broken your heart? What can you do to make peace with what happened?

- What can you tell yourself the next time you need to put things in perspective?

- When was the last time you cried?

- Is there someone in your life around whom you have to walk on eggshells? What truth do you have to face about that relationship?

- What painful event in your life led to greater wisdom?

- Whom will you disappoint? Why? Can this be avoided? If so, how?

- What current crisis is actually an opportunity? What is your next step?

Four of Swords

- How do you currently recharge your batteries? What new ways of recharging your batteries can you try out?

- What loose ends do you need to tie up?

- From what or whom do you need a break? How will you take it?

- What part of your physical body do you need to heal? How will you go about doing so?

- How are you planning for your future?

- What do you do to ensure that you don't get stuck in your head?

- Is it time to take a "mental health day"? How might you do so without feeling guilty? What would your mental health day consist of?

- Do you currently practice meditation or another type of mindfulness practice? If not, would you be willing to explore the benefits of doing so?

- What role does prayer play in your life? If you were to write a personal prayer, what would it say?

- What is a gift you can give yourself this week? This month? This year?

- Why might it be time to re-examine some of your long-held ideas about the world and your place in it?

- What is hanging over your head? What can you do to remove that issue or worry?

- How do you make sure your self-talk doesn't overwhelm or discourage you? Is there a skill you could learn that would help with that?

- What is your source of support during difficult times?

- Whom would you like to help? Why? What is your first step toward doing so?

- Why might it be time to reinvent yourself? What would be the result of that transformation?

- What needs to be your main priority? Why?

- Why might it be a good time to step back and review the course of your life? What would you include in that review?

- What worked out well during this past year? What didn't?

- Do you typically take breaks during the day? If not, why might that be a good idea?

Five of Swords

- How have things gone wrong?

- What do you just feel awful about?

- What isn't working out?

- How has someone taken advantage of you?

- Who or what do you need to walk away from?

- How can you best protect yourself from a toxic situation or relationship?

- What is confusing you? How can you gain clarity?

- What argument do you know you'll never win?

- To whom are you lying? Why?

- How are you being deceitful? What are the possible consequences?

- How are you winning? Do you have a clear conscience?

- Whom have you hurt? How can you make amends?

- How are you being careful in terms of how you speak to others? Why might that be important?

- How are you making the people around you feel?

- Why might it be a good idea to connect with your sense of humility?

- How are you treating yourself? Do you ever engage in self-destructive behavior? Why? How might you begin to show yourself compassion and kindness?

- How are you treating those around you who have less power?

- What situation has become untenable? What is the way out? What price are you willing to pay to exit?

- What does it means to have "integrity"? How is your life aligned with your personal values? If your life is not currently aligned with what you value, what are the next steps you must take in order to create that alignment?

- What might backfire? What is your backup?

- What do you need to push through?

- About what do you need to act more aggressively? Why?

- How are you choosing your battles?

- What toxic person or situation do you need to avoid? How can you best do so?

Six of Swords

- What have you been putting off? Why?

- What chapter is closing in your life? What chapter is beginning? How might you honor this transition?

- Who has been your mentor? How might you show them your gratitude?

- Let's assume you have a guardian angel. What do they look like? Sound like? What message do they have for you?

- Who do you go to when times get tough? How do they help?

- How might you strengthen your support system?

- From what is it time to depart?

- How are you healing?

- What is the nature of your self-talk? Is it typically empowering or does it cause you suffering?

- How clear are your plans for the future?

- What is getting in the way of clarity? How might you regain your focus?

- How easy is it for you to manage your thoughts?

- How are you developing your power of attention and focus?

- What is changing in your life?

- What are you resisting? Why? What are the benefits of doing so?

- How can you best honor your child self? How can you best honor your teenage self?

- What allows you to think clearly? How can you ensure that you are thinking clearly the next time you have to make a decision?

- How are you keeping yourself grounded?

- What inner journey is it necessary for you to take? Why?

- Why might a change of scenery be beneficial?

- What makes you sad? Why?

- What do you need to start over?

- Whom or what do you miss? How can you honor those memories?

- Whom must you forgive in order to move forward in your life?

Seven of Swords

- How are you being proactive?

- How are you protecting your interests?

- How are you operating under the radar? Why is that a good idea? How will you know when to make yourself known?

- What risk are you running? Why will it be worth it? What is your Plan B?

- What dangerous game are you playing?

- What problem do you need to explore from a different angle? What would be some creative ways of looking for solutions?

- How are you holding yourself back?

- What is distracting you?

- How can you best prepare for what's just around the corner?

- What situation do you need to exit? How can you do so gracefully?

- What are you forgetting?

- Of what or whom should you be skeptical? Why?

- How can you ensure that you are going in the right direction?

- How are you developing your adaptability...your flexibility?

- Who is a threat? What is your best defense?

- What could backfire? What is your backup plan?

- What is your relationship with Trust? How did it develop? How might you improve it?

- What is your hidden agenda?

- In what area of your life might it be best to act alone? Why?

- How are you operating outside of a community? Is that a good idea?

- What might you come to regret?

- Is there something from your past that could catch up with you? How can you protect yourself?

- What is your gut telling you? What is your next step?

- What do you need to deal with instead of avoid? How does this relate to being courageous?

Eight of Swords

- How are you feeling trapped? How did you get to this point? What is your next step?

- Over what or whom are you obsessing? Why? What is that energy drain keeping you from doing?

- How are you limiting yourself?

- How are you letting other people's judgments impact you?

- What matters do you need to take into your own hands?

- How have you abdicated your responsibility? What do you need to take responsibility for?

- How are you living in your head? What have been the consequences of doing so?

- How are you stuck? What will being unstuck feel like? What is the next step?

- What feeling are you ignoring? Why?

- What are you assuming? What can you do to investigate that assumption to see if it is valid or not?

- How are you a victim?

- How might you use your creativity to solve a pressing issue?

- How are you ignoring your sensual side? What can you do to honor it more regularly?

- What has withered inside you? How might you rejuvenate it?

- How are your fears holding you back? What can you do in order to move through them?

- How are you sabotaging yourself? Why might you being doing that?

- How have you lost your way? What is your first step back home?

- What are you homesick for? Why do you think that is?

- How are you listening to your intuition? How might you hear your intuitive voice more clearly?

- How might a trip (either short or long-term) change your way of thinking? Where would you go?

- What does it mean to be powerful? How are you powerful? What can you do to connect even more deeply with your personal power?

  What do you need to believe?

Nine of Swords

- In what crisis do you find yourself? Who can you turn to for help?

- What are you over-thinking? How might you find a better sense of balance?

- What keeps you up at night? Where will find the solution?

- What do you need to accept? What can you tell yourself that would make doing that easier?

- What do you need to release? How might you do so most effectively?

- What daily cleansing or purification rituals do you engage in? Why might those be a good idea for you?

- What are you favorite ways of grounding or centering yourself?

- What new skill do you need to learn in order to sleep more soundly?

- Who or what is draining your energy? What can you do to minimize those energy drains?

- Who or what do you fear? What is your next step?

- What are you doing each day in order to replenish your energy?

- What is your relationship with energy work (such as Reiki)? How might you develop that relationship?

- What is hanging over your head? What do you need to do about it?

- What are your deepest regrets? What can you do to begin to heal so that you do not carry them with you for the rest of your life?

- How do you challenge negative self-talk? Is there a new skill you need to learn or book you should read that will help?

- How are you addressing your anxiety? What skills do you need to develop to better manage it?

- Who or what do you need to mourn? Are you willing to give yourself the time and space to do so?

- How are you creating security for yourself in case hard times come?

- What mistake have you made? How can you make it right?

- Are you being too hard on yourself? How would you know?

Ten of Swords

- How are you coping? What can you do to better develop your coping skills?

- Who or what are you done with? Why?

- What is bottoming out in your life? What is your next step?

- Why might it be a good idea for you to take a mental health day?

- What chapter in your life needs to end in order for a new (and better) one to begin?

- How have you been too trusting? What have been the results?

- Who has betrayed you? How? How can you heal from your hurt?

- What patterns do you notice in your life? (think in terms of relationships; family life; money; work/career; physical and mental health)

- Are there any patterns in your life that you need to change? How might you best go about doing so?

- How has being "nice" to other people caused you suffering?

- Is there a difference between being "nice" and being "kind"? How might being kind be more empowering and healthy than being nice?

- Do you consider yourself a "people pleaser"? If so, why? What can you do in order to become more assertive?

- Why might it be time to reinvent yourself? Please describe the "new you." What would be the first step in that direction?

- How has your belief system disempowered you? Where did you learn those beliefs? With what might you replace them?

- How easy is it for you to be spontaneous? What holds you back? Why might more spontaneity improve your quality of life?

- What childhood needs were not met by your parents? How can you now, as an adult, meet those needs?

- Who or what gives you hope for the future?

- How do you typically pull yourself out of a rut? Do you need to learn some new strategies for doing so? What might those be?

- About what do you need to "expect the best but prepare for the worst"?

Page of Swords

- What is something new you'd like to learn? Why? How will you go about doing so?

- What does it mean to be "mentally disciplined"? Why is this an important skill to have? How might you develop it?

- What large project or problem do you need to break down into smaller chunks?

- How are you out of your depth? What can you do to remedy the situation?

- Are you spending too much time in your head? How can you connect more with your spiritual side? Your emotional side? Your fun side?

- What does the idea that "You are not your thoughts" mean to you?

- How are you developing a mindfulness practice? Why might that be a good idea?

- Who should you be going to for advice?

- How are you keeping yourself grounded?

- What strategy or strategies do you use to stop yourself from ruminating? Are there any you need to learn?

- About what do you need more information? From where will you get it?

- Where is your curiosity leading you?

- What is a social cause that is close to your heart? How might you lend your support to it?

- What current problem do you need to look at from another angle?

- Do you feel that you are a good listener? How do you know?

- Do you have a good conversation partner? If not, how might you find one?

- What is something about which you should be more realistic?

- Who or what do you need to be watching more carefully?

- With whom do you need to have an honest conversation? Why? What would you say?

- What do you look forward to each day?

- What new project is it time to start? How can you set yourself up for success?

- Who should you ally yourself with?

Knight of Swords

- How are you developing expertise? Why might mastery of a particular skill or topic be a good idea?

- In what area of your life must you slow down?

- What do you need to really think through?

- To what are you committed? Why?

- What are you overthinking?

- How can you develop your charisma?

- How attentive are you to the impact your words and actions have on others?

- About what do you need to trust your intuition?

- How can you be certain you are moving in the right direction?

- How might your emotions be getting in your way? What can you do to better manage them?

- About what should you be more open-minded? Why?

- How are you undervaluing yourself? What can you do in order to get what you deserve?

- How is guilt impacting your life? What do you need to do in order to release it?

- How can you learn to be more sensitive to the needs of others? To your own needs?

- What is something you would like to share with others? Why? How might you best do so?

- How can you best get out of your own way? Why is this a good idea?

- How might you be barking up the wrong tree? What is a better alternative?

- What price are you paying for living life on your own terms? Is it worth it? Why?

- About what are you absolutely sure? How do you know?

- How are you forcing an issue? Is that a good idea?

- Are you cutting corners? Why might you eventually regret doing so?

- Have you found your community? If not, what is the first step towards doing so?

- About what should you be more patient? Why?

- Who is wasting your time? What is your next step?

Queen of Swords

- What are you tolerating in your life? Why? Is there something you need to do about it?

- Is it easy for you to be critical of others? What are the consequences of doing so?

- Where do you go / what do you do in order to clear your mind?

- What do you need to take less seriously? Why?

- What do you need to take more seriously? Why?

- How do you typically make decisions?

- How does fear influence how you make decisions? How does love?

- About what do you you need to take the high road? Why?

- How are you ensuring that your judgements are unclouded by bias or ignorance?

- How might self-discipline give you more freedom? What would be a way for your develop that discipline?

- How are you stuck? What can you do to free yourself?

- Who or what do you need to face head-on? What will give you the courage you need to do what you have to do?

- What truth must you accept? How can you do so with equanimity?

- How are you protecting your integrity?

- What are your expectations for the future? How can you best manifest them?

- How can you best ensure that you are being realistic about the future?

- With whom do you need to have a conversation? Why is it important to do this sooner rather than later?

- Who or what do you need to put to rest? Why?

- How have you grown over the past year? What is your plan for personal growth for the coming year?

- How are you avoiding pettiness?

- How are you living into your full potential? What must you do in order to continue to move in that direction?

- Whom do you need to convince? Why? What is your best strategy for doing so?

King of Swords

- Why might it be a good idea to simplify your life? How might you go about doing so?

- What is your philosophy of life?

- For whom are you seeking justice? Why? What would be the most effective way of doing so?

- On what issue is it imperative that you see all sides? Why?

- How are you keeping your mind sharp?

- Of what are you a master? How did you reach that point?

- What is something you would like to learn? Why?

- How are you minimizing the drama in your life?

- What are your plans for the future? How are you ensuring that they will come to pass?

- What book do you have in you?

- What are your core values? How is your daily life aligned with those values? If your life is not fully aligned with those values, what do you need to change?

- What price are you willing to pay to honor your integrity? Why?

- What can you do to show yourself compassion and kindness?

- How are you sharing your widsom with others?

- What has life taught you?

- What advice would you give your younger self?

- Do you feel you are living your full potential? If not, what do you have to do to begin to move in that direction?

- How have you changed over the past five years? How do those changes make you feel?

- When do you feel most alive?

- What are you doing to avoid boredom?

- From where or whom do you get advice? Might there be another source that would also be helpful?

- In what current situation is it vital for you to remain objective?

- Whom do you need to "call out"? How can you most effectively do so?

Ace of Pentacles

- How are you saving for the future?

- What seeds are you planting?

- What are you doing to take care of your body?

- What excites you about the future?

- How is your relationship with food? Is there something you can do to improve it?

- What is your favorite smell or secent? How can you incorporate it regularly into your life?

- Who or what makes you smile?

- What kind of music energizes you? Relaxes you? How might you add more music into your life?

- How important is touch to you? Why or why not?

- What resources do you need to cultivate in order to achieve your goals?

- What gift should you accept? What is a gift you can give to someone else this week?

- How can you best express gratitude for what you currently have in your life?

- How are you sleeping? How can you improve the quality of your sleep?

- Why might it be a good idea to slow down and appreciate what is around you?

- Do you feel your life is in balance? If not, how might you begin to move in that direction?

- In what direction are you being pulled?

- Why might it be a good idea to explore the natural world more deeply?

- What gift have you been ignoring?

- About what should you be more realistic?

- What can you do in order to feel more secure?

- How do you like to recharge your batteries?

- How can you add meaning to your life?

- What would be the best way for you to invest in your personal development this year?

- How are you growing your nest egg?

- What is something you should add to your life? Why would that be a good idea?

Two of Pentacles

- What is your secret to success?

- What role does sensuality play in your life?

- What keeps you grounded?

- Is there anything out of balance in your life? If so, what is your next step?

- How are you having fun?

- What is something you've always wanted to try? What is your next step?

- To what must you adapt?

- Are your priorities in the right order? How do you know?

- When times are tough, what can you tell yourself that will help you cope?

- How are you being pulled in opposite directions? What is the remedy?

- How are you managing your time? What can you do to better manage it?

- From what is it time to take a break?

- What does it mean to you to "go with the flow"? Why might this be a good thing for you to do?

- What goal do you temporarily have to put on the back burner? Why?

- What area of your life have you been ignoring? Why?

- What is your definition of success? How is it currently playing out in your life?

- How can you best avoid distractions?

- With what or whom must you be patient?

- What is a something you would like to master? How can you best ensure your commitment to the process of mastery?

- What is your relationship with money?

- How are you managing your money? What, if anything, needs to change?

- How are you adapting yourself to changing times?

- About what should you have more of a sense of humor?

- How can you best embrace the fact that life is uncertain?

Three of Pentacles

- What do you want to manifest in the world? Why? What would your first step be?

- What are you currently building? How is it going?

- Can you trust the people you are depending on? How do you know?

- How open are you to feedback? Why is this necessary?

- What roles are you currently playing in your life? Is there one that you need to clarify?

- What are you planning to do? How clear is your motivation?

- How deliberate are you when it comes to your physical health? Mental health?

- How are you treating your body? What is one change you might consider making?

- What gift can you give your body? Why?

- With whom should you collaborate? What are the benefits of doing so?

- On what is it time to put the finishing touches so you can move on?

- What is the role of spirituality in your life? Why might it be a good idea to develop or deepen a spiritual practice?

- How are you keeping your mind/body/spirit in balance?

- To whom should you go for advice? Why might that be a priority at this time?

- How are you being pulled in different directions? What is the solution?

- About what should you be expecting the best but also preparing for the worst?

- How do you keep yourself motivated when you are in the middle of a project? Is there an ally you can go to who will hold you accountable when necessary? How would that be a benefit?

- How are you preparing for potential problems?

- What should you be paying attention to?

- What should you be deferring to an expert? Where might you find such a person?

- Who do you want on your team? Why? Who do you need to kick off your team? Why?

- How will attention to detail pay off in the long run?

Four of Pentacles

- What are you afraid of?

- What is your philosophy of money? What is its purpose?

- Are your decisions typically fear-based or love-based?

- What part of you is stagnating? How can you get it moving again?

- What are you resisting? Why?

- What are you holding onto that you should really let go of?

- How are your material possessions owning you? How do they restrict your life? Your energy?

- What are you afraid of losing? How might that fear be making things worse?

- What chapter needs to close in your life? Why?

- What gets your energy moving? How can you incorporate more of that into your life?

- About what do you need to loosen up?

- How might a personal weakness also be a strength?

- What in your life is a losing battle? What do you need to accept about it so you can move on?

- What scares you about being vulnerable?

- How might being vulnerable lead to healing? How can you learn to be more vulnerable?

- How might sharing a secret lead to a positive outcome?

- What does it mean to have an "abundance mindset"? How might such a perspective be beneficial to you?

- How are you protecting your heart?

- How are you keeping yourself grounded?

- How are can you best avoid taking on other people's crap?

- What boundary do you need to strengthen? Why?

- How are you trapped? What can you do to free yourself?

- How do you measure your success?

- What is the last thing you think about at night before falling asleep? What is on your mind when you wake up in the morning?

Five of Pentacles

- Where are you going? Do you know why you are headed in that direction? Or have you forgotten?

- What source of support are you overlooking?

- What do you need in order to be fulfilled in your life? (make a list) How are each of those needs currently being met? What changes must you make in order to adequately meet each of your needs?

- How have you been rejected? What can you do in order to heal from that pain?

- Do you feel part of a community? If not, what steps do you need to take to find your tribe?

- How are you paying attention to your physical needs?

- What does it mean to feel "burned out"? Are you feeling burned out? If so, what is the remedy? What message do you think that feeling is sending?

- Do you feel grateful for what you have? Why is gratitude important? What might you do to develop or increase that sense of appreciation?

- How are you suffering? What might you do to begin to decrease your pain?

- What don't you see? How would seeing it change everything?

- Whom are you following? How do you know that you can trust them?

- What makes you feel alive? How can you maximize its presence in your life?

- How are you connecting with your spirituality? Why might this type of connection be a good idea? What spiritual practice should you explore?

- What are you running away from? How can you be sure it is a good idea to do so? What would happen if you stopped running?

- About what should you remind yourself: "This too shall pass"?

- Whom should you be supporting? How can you best do so?

- What lessons have you learned? What will you do differently the next time?

- How do you measure your self-worth? Is that something that needs to change?

- Have you ever found yourself in a desperate situation? How did you recover?

Six of Pentacles

- What aspect of yourself have you been ignoring? Why?

- How are you being denied? How can you mitigate your suffering?

- Upon whom or what are you dependent? How does that dependence make you feel? How can you gain your independence?

- For whom or what have you been waiting? If you are honest with yourself, is it going to be worth the wait?

- How can you best avoid being at the mercy of another? How can you become self-sufficient?

- What is it you want? What price are you willing to pay for it? Why?

- How have you sold yourself out? That is, how have you compromised your integrity? Was it worth it?

- How has life treated you unfairly? How can you heal from that pain?

- How is your patience being tested?

- What are you ashamed of? How might you release that shame?

- How are you settling? Why are you doing so?

- How are you limiting your full potential?

- How is fear constraining your life?

- How are you serving others? Whom would you like to serve? Why? How can you best do so?

- What role does power play in your life? What role would you like it to play?

- Why might it be a positive experience for you to become a mentor?

- Where is your energy going?

- How can you ensure that your decision-making process is informed by love?

- How are you sharing your gifts?

- Who or what deserves your mercy? Why?

- How are you balancing the energy that comes into your life with the energy that you expend each day?

- Are you feeling un- or underappreciated? What do you need to do next?

- How equal are your relationships with others?

Seven of Pentacles

- How have things been going?

- What investment has paid off? What do you think your next investment should be?

- What can you do to celebrate a recent success?

- Are you satisfied with your progress? If not, what needs to change?

- How are you taking time to pause and reflect?

- In what should you invest more time and energy? Why?

- How are you following (and honoring) the rhythms of life?

- Where should you go next?

- Do you have a super-power that you are overlooking?

- How are you appreciating what you have?

- How are you laying the groundwork for your next success?

- How can you ensure that you are moving at just the right speed?

- Have your efforts been worthwhile? Why or why not?

- Is there an area in your life in which you need to slow down?

- How far have you come?

- What does the next chapter of your life hold?

- Who or what do you need to weed out of your life?

- At what crossroads do you stand? What needs to happen in order for you to take your next step?

- How are you frustrated? In what should you continue to persevere?

- What must you re-evaluate? Why?

- Whom or what deserves your attention and care?

- How can you best protect your savings?

- How are you taking care of your body?

- How are you reviewing what has been working in your life and what needs improvement?

- How are you prioritizing your activities? What needs to take priority in your life?

Eight of Pentacles

- What is your mission in life? How do you know? How are you serving that mission?

- How attentive are you to detail? Why might this kind of attention be a good idea?

- What is your relationship with perfectionism? How does perfeccionism disempower you? What can you do about it?

- Of what would you consider yourself a master or expert? Please describe how you reached that point.

- To whom or what are you committed? Why? How are you demonstrating your commitment?

- What skill are you currently in the process of mastering? Which strategies are you using? How are they working out for you?

- How are you balancing work with the other areas of your life? Does anything need to change? Why?

- How are you isolating yourself? Is this a good idea? What might be some of the negative consequences of your isolation? Positive consequences?

- Over whom or what are you obsessing? How is this obsession impacting your life? What might you do to give yourself a break?

- What are you doing to improve the quality of your life?

- When do you feel most most "in the zone"? When time is standing still and you're completely absorbed in what you're doing?

- How are you distracting yourself from what is important?

- How are your relationships with family and friends? Does anything need to improve? If so, how might you go about doing so?

- Could a mentor be helpful at this point in your life? If so, how might you find one?

- How is your dedication paying off?

- How do you feel about mentoring another person? How might doing so positively impact their life? Your life?

- What aspect of your life have you outgrown? How do you know? What is your next step?

- What do you love doing?

- What is a skill you would like to learn? Why?

- How can you create the time and space you need for creative work?

Nine of Pentacles

- About what do you feel supremely confident? Why?

- In terms of your five senses, what can you do to luxuriate in each?

- How are you in control? How does it feel?

- How has your patience paid off?

- What role does timing need to play in your life right now?

- How are you honoring those who helped you on your road to success?

- Why might it be a good idea to review the foundations of your skills?

- What role does luxury play in your life? How might you create luxurious experiences for yourself that are not dependent on money?

- On what should you splurge? Why?

- How are you enjoying what you have? How are you appreciating what you have?

- How are you meeting your needs? Are there any that require special attention at this point in time?

- What does the term "personal power" mean to you? How connected are you to your sense of personal power? How might you develop and strengthen that connection?

- Are you feeling at ease? If not, what can you do in order to experience more of that in your life?

- What is your favorite pastime? Why?

- Are you comfortable being in solitude? If not, why might it be a good idea to learn how to be?

- How are you protecting yourself? How are you protectings those who you love?

- How are you enjoying your success?

- How are you ensuring that your future will be secure?

- How are you paying attention to the little things in life? Why might that be a good idea?

- How can you ensure that what you love doesn't harm or kill you? How can you ensure that you don't kill what you love?

- What is your relationship with nature? Why might it be a good idea to deepen that relationship?

- How has self-discipline impacted your success?

Ten of Pentacles

- What new family tradition should you begin? Why? What about a personal tradition (for you alone)? Why might it be a good idea to add one to your life?

- What current traditions feel good? Why? How do they enrich your life?

- What tradition or traditions should you put to rest? Why?

- What hidden gem is in your midst? How can you find it in order to utilize its powers?

- How are you thinking about your future? How are you preparing for your future?

- How comfortable are you with the idea of impermanence?

- How comfortable are you with the fact of your own mortality?

- What are you doing now that will allow you to die without regret?

- How are you connecting with a younger generation? Why might that be a good idea?

- How are you relaxing into your success?

- Why might it be a good idea to seek out wisdom from an older person?

- What do you see that others don't?

- What does the concept of "home" mean to you?

- Whom are you ignoring? Why might that not be such a good idea?

- What threshold are you about to step over? How have you prepared for what is to come next?

- How will you know when you've succeeded? What would your next step then be?

- Whom or what are you responsible for? How has that been working out?

- What did your parents teach you about the world around you? Your place in the world? Your self-worth?

- What past hurt must you release in order to move forward in your life?

- What would you like your legacy to be? What epitaph would you want on your tombstone?

Page of Pentacles

- How are you acting on your dreams? If you aren't...what is getting in the way?

- What is your body telling you? What is your next step?

- What do you crave? Why do you think that is?

- What new habit should you start? Why?

- How can you experience the joy of being alive?

- Where is your sense of wonder? How can you foster it?

- What is your definition of success?

- How much money do you need to be happy?

- How can you become more comfortable in your body?

- What do you enjoy collecting? Why?

- What might be fun to begin collecting? Why?

- What collection of yours is it time to part with? Why might that be a good idea?

- What are your ambitions? What do you hope to gain?

- Where do you want to end up in 5 years? What are you doing today that will lead you in that direction?

- How are you frustrated? Why do you think that is? What is your next step?

- What role does patience need to play in your life? Why?

- How are you tending to what is yours?

- How can you ensure that you stay on your chosen path?

- What is distracting you?

- What gift can you give your body?

- About what must you be more diligent?

- How can you grow your nest egg?

- How can you explore your sensuality?

- What aspect of your sexuality needs attention?

- What should you re-evaluate?

Knight of Pentacles

- What are you waiting for?

- What should you reconsider?

- What do you need to see through? Why?

- About what are you being too cautious?

- What is something you need to quit? Why?

- How are you blocked? What is the next step?

- What has slowed down in your life? Is it a positive or negative thing? Why?

- Are you willing to pay the price to remain true to yourself?

- What compromise should you make? Why?

- What do you need to double-check?

- What do you need to risk?

- How are you strengthening your core?

- How are you missing out? What is the remedy?

- What is something you are afraid of doing? Why is it important for you to go ahead and face your fear?

- What is something you need to finally complete and be done with?

- How can you develop your optimistic side?

- How can you incorporate more play into your life?

- What are you doing for fun?

- For what are you gathering your strength? Where will your energy come from? How will you renew it?

- How are you protecting yourself? Why is that necessary?

- How can you best develop your flexibility?

- How are you laying the foundations of your future?

- About what should you be more cautious?

- What makes you dependable? Why is that important?

- In what area of your life is moderation the key? In what area is it a good time to go to the extreme?

Queen of Pentacles

- How are you creating a home for yourself?

- How are you ensuring that you live in a warm, welcoming environment?

- Whom are you nurturing?

- How can you better care for your body?

- How are you being generous?

- Whom or what deserves your undivided attention? Why?

- How are you honoring each of your senses?

- What are your daily strategies for centering yourself?

- How are you taking time for yourself?

- How can you best heal from your past hurts?

- What is your relationship with nature?

- How are you surrounding yourself with beauty?

- How are you honoring your sensuality?

- How might you connect more deeply with the animal world?

- What or whom do you need to welcome into your life?

- Whom must you support? How might you best show that support?

- How can you nurture your inner child?

- What can you do to ensure that your home environment is safe?

- What can you do to maintain the blessings in your life?

- What secret have you been carrying? Why? What is it time to do with it?

- How are you staying out of debt?

- Who are you taking care of?

- How can you ensure that you have the necessary time to recharge your batteries?

- How can make certain that your career doesn't consume you and/or your family?

King of Pentacles

- How are you maximizing your opportunities?

- How are you protecting your assets?

- How are you protecting yourself?

- How are you balancing the material with the spiritual?

- How are you celebrating the results of your hard work?

- How confident are you? What fulels your confidence? Is there anything you need to do to develop it?

- Of what are you proud? Why?

- What lessons have you learned?

- How are you sharing your knowledge with others?

- How are you treating yourself with respect?

- What is a gift you can give to another?

- How can you share your resources with others? Why might this be a good idea?

- What role does power play in your life?

- What is the big picture?

- What past decisions have brought you to your current position?

- How are you generating energy for yourself? For others?

- How are you keeping yourself up-to-date?

- How much control do you have over your time? Why is it important to have such control?

- Whom do you need to encourage? Why?

- How did you remain true to yourself?

- How did you make a difference in the world?

- What are three of your favorite sayings?

- What is your motto?

- How have you proven yourself?

- What are you best known for? What would you like to be known for?

About the Author

Andy Matzner is a licensed clinical social worker and psychotherapist. He also teaches psychology at Virginia Western Community College and gender and women's studies at Hollins University. Andy is also the author of several books, including *The Tarot Activity Book: A collection of creative and therapeutic ideas for the cards.*

Made in the USA
Coppell, TX
07 March 2024